PRAYERFULLY

Poems of Devotion

Helen Steiner Rice

PRAYERFULLY

Poems of Devotion

Decorations by Biro

Hutchinson
London Sydney Auckland Johannesburg

© Author 1971 Fleming H. Revell Company
© Drawings 1971 Hutchinson Ltd

The right of Helen Steiner Rice to be identified as Author of
this work has been asserted by Helen Steiner Rice in accordance
with the Copyright, Designs and Patents Act, 1988.

This edition first published in 1972 by Hutchinson
Second impression January 1973
Third impression May 1974
Fourth impression May 1976
Fifth impression September 1977
Sixth impression February 1980
Seventh impression September 1981
Eighth impression October 1982
Ninth impression March 1985
Tenth impression April 1986
Eleventh impression April 1987
Twelfth impression January 1990
Thirteenth impression October 1990

Random Century Group Ltd
20 Vauxhall Bridge Road, London SW1V 2SA

Random Century Australia (Pty) Ltd
20 Alfred Street, Milsons Point, Sydney, NSW 2061, Australia

Random Century New Zealand Ltd
PO Box 40–086, Glenfield, Auckland 10, New Zealand

Random Century South Africa (Pty) Ltd
PO Box 337, Bergvlei, 2012, South Africa

ISBN 0 09 113830 2

Printed and bound in Great Britain by
Biddles Ltd, Guildford and King's Lynn

Foreword

It is a special pleasure to add this volume of devotional verses to those other volumes by Helen Steiner Rice, already published in Britain—*Just For You*, *Heart Gifts* and *Lovingly*.

This gifted woman does not *write* her poems, she always insists; she simply shares what she is given. Her work appeals to all sorts and conditions of men and women, in many different countries, for it strikes the deep notes of spiritual reality undergirding the world. What she has to say about prayer is in the language common to all who seek that reality. Much of her verse is born of the trouble and turmoil that comes to everyone. The difference is that Mrs. Rice has learnt to cope with every kind of problem in serenity and triumph. No wonder someone said that she "talks about God as if he were right at her elbow".

It comes as no surprise then to learn that every morning Helen Steiner Rice rises early and offers a special prayer which "gives me strength and courage to meet the frustrations and discouragements that lie ahead. I say it each morning as I watch God usher in another day and gently tuck the night away!"

This is her prayer:
Bless me, heavenly Father,
    Forgive my erring ways,
Grant me strength to serve Thee,
    Put purpose in my days . . .
Give me understanding
    Enough to make me kind
So I may judge all people
    With my heart and not my mind . . .
And teach me to be patient
    In everything I do,
Content to trust Your wisdom
    And to follow after You . . .
And help me when I falter
    And hear me when I pray
And receive me in Thy Kingdom
    To dwell with Thee some day.

Good Morning, God!

You are ushering in another day
Untouched and freshly new
So here I come to ask You, God,
If You'll renew me, too,
Forgive the many errors
That I made yesterday
And let me try again, dear God,
To walk closer in Thy way . . .
But, Father, I am well aware
I can't make it on my own
So take my hand and hold it tight
For I can't walk alone!

It's Me Again, God

Remember me, God?
I come every day
Just to talk with You, Lord,
And to learn how to pray . . .
You make me feel welcome,
You reach out Your hand,
I need never explain
For You understand . . .
I come to You frightened
And burdened with care
So lonely and lost
And so filled with despair,
And suddenly, Lord,
I'm no longer afraid,
My burden is lighter
And the dark shadows fade . . .
Oh, God, what a comfort
To know that You care
And to know when I seek You
You will always be there!

Daily Prayers Are "Heaven's Stairs"

The Stairway rises Heaven High—
The Steps are dark and steep,
In weariness we climb them
As we stumble, fall and weep . . .
And many times we falter
Along the "path of prayer"
Wondering if You hear us
And if You really care . . .
Oh, give us some assurance,
Restore our faith anew,
So we can keep on climbing
The Stairs of Prayer to you—
For we are weak and wavering,
Uncertain and unsure,
And only meeting You in prayer
Can help us to endure
All life's trials and troubles
Its sickness, pain and sorrow,
And give us strength and courage
To face and meet Tomorrow!

What Is Prayer?

Is it measured words that are memorized,
Forcefully said and dramatized,
Offered with pomp and with arrogant pride
In words unmatched to the feelings inside?
No . . . prayer is so often just words unspoken
Whispered in tears by a heart that is broken . . .
For God is already deeply aware
Of the burdens we find too heavy to bear,
And all we need do is to seek Him in prayer
And without a word He will help us to bear
Our trials and troubles—our sickness and sorrow
And show us the way to a brighter tomorrow . . .
There's no need at all for impressive prayer
For the minute we seek God He is already there!

God, Are You There?

I'm way down here!
You're way up there!
Are You sure You can hear
My faint, faltering prayer?
For I'm so unsure
Of just how to pray—
To tell you the truth, God,
I don't know what to say . . .
I just know I am lonely
And vaguely disturbed,
Bewildered and restless,
Confused and perturbed . . .
And they tell me that prayer
Helps to quiet the mind
And to unburden the heart
For in stillness we find
A newborn assurance
That someone does care
And someone does answer
Each small sincere prayer!

The Mystery of Prayer

Beyond that which words can interpret
Or theology can explain
The soul feels a shower of refreshment
That falls like the gentle rain
On hearts that are parched with problems
And are searching to find the way
To somehow attract God's attention
Through well-chosen words as they pray,
Not knowing that God in His wisdom
Can sense all man's worry and woe
For there is nothing man can conceal
That God does not already know . . .
So kneel in prayer in His presence
And you'll find no need to speak
For softly in silent communion
God grants you the peace that you seek.

No Favour Do I Seek Today

I come not to ask, to plead or implore You,
I just come to tell You how much I adore You,
For to kneel in Your Presence makes me feel blest
For I know that You know all my needs best . . .
And it fills me with joy just to linger with You
As my soul You replenish and my heart You renew,
For prayer is much more than just asking for things—
It's the peace and contentment that quietness brings . . .
So thank You again for Your mercy and love
And for making me heir to Your kingdom above!

My Garden of Prayer

My garden beautifies my yard
    and adds fragrance to the air . . .
But it is also my cathedral
    and my quiet place of prayer . . .
So little do we realize
    that the glory and the power
Of He who made the Universe
    lies hidden in a flower.

"What Has Been Is What Will Be ... and There Is Nothing New Under the Sun"

(ECCLESIASTES 1:9)

Today my soul is reaching out
For something that's unknown,
I cannot grasp or fathom it
For it's known to God alone—
I cannot hold or harness it
Or put it into form,
For it's as uncontrollable
As the wind before the storm—
I know not where it came from
Or whither it will go,
For it's as inexplicable
As the restless winds that blow—
And like the wind it too will pass
And leave nothing more behind
Than the memory of a mystery
That blew across my mind—
But like the wind it will return
To keep reminding me
That everything that has been
Is what again will be—
For there is nothing that is new
Beneath God's timeless sun,
And present, past and future
Are all moulded into one—

And east and west and north and south
The same wind keeps on blowing,
While rivers run on endlessly
Yet the sea's not overflowing—
And the restless unknown longing
Of my searching soul won't cease
Until God comes in glory
And my soul at last finds peace.

Finding Faith in a Flower

Sometimes when faith is running low
And I cannot fathom why things are so . . .
I walk alone among the flowers I grow
And learn the "answers" to all I would know!
For among my flowers I have come to see
Life's miracle and its mystery . . .
And standing in silence and reverie
My faith comes flooding back to me!

God, Grant Me the Glory
of "Thy Gift"

God, widen my vision so I may see
    the afflictions You have sent to me—
Not as a cross too heavy to wear
    that weights me down in gloomy despair—
Not as something to hate and despise
    but a gift of love sent in disguise—
Something to draw me closer to You
    to teach me patience and forbearance, too—
Something to show me more clearly the way
    to serve You and love You more every day—
Something priceless and precious and rare
    that will keep me forever safe in Thy care
Aware of the spiritual strength that is mine
    if my selfish, small will is lost in Thine!

Don't Let Me Falter

Oh Lord, don't let me falter—
    Don't let me lose my way;
Don't let me cease to carry
    My burden, day be day . . .
Oh Lord, don't let me stumble—
    Don't let me fall and quit . . .
Oh Lord, please help me find my "job"
    And help me shoulder it.

A Prayer for Patience

God, teach me to be patient—
Teach me to go slow—
Teach me how to "wait on You"
When my way I do not know . . .
Teach me sweet forbearance
When things do not go right
So I remain unruffled
When others grow "uptight" . . .
Teach me how to quiet
My racing, rising heart
So I may hear the answer
You are trying to impart . . .
Teach me to let go, dear God,
And pray undisturbed until
My heart is filled with inner peace
And I learn to know Your will!

God, Are You Really Real?

I want to believe
I want to be true
I want to be loyal
And faithful to You,
But where can I go
When vague doubts arise
And when evil appears
In an angel's disguise
While clamouring voices
Demand my attention
And the air is polluted
With cries of dissension,
You know, God, it's easy
Just to follow the crowd
Who are "doing their thing"
While shouting out loud
Gross protestations
Against the "old rules"
That limit and hamper
The new freedom schools . . .
God, answer this prayer
And tell me the truth—
Are YOU really the God
Of both Age and of Youth?
And, God speak to my heart
So I truly feel
That these "prophets" are false
But YOU REALLY ARE REAL!

Make Me a Channel of Blessing Today

"Make me a channel of blessing today."
I ask again and again when I pray . . .
Do I turn a deaf ear to the Master's voice
Or refuse to heed His directions and choice?
I know at the end of the day
That I did so little to pay my way!

The Answer

In the tiny petal
    of a tiny flower
        that grew from a tiny pod . . .
Is the miracle
    and the mystery
        of all Creation and God!

Open My Eyes

God open my eyes
    so I may see
And feel Your presence
    close to me . . .
Give me strength
    for my stumbling feet
As I battle the crowd
    on life's busy street,
And widen the vision
    of my unseeing eyes
So in passing faces
    I'll recognize
Not just a stranger,
    unloved and unknown,
But a friend with a heart
    that is much like my own . . .
Give me perception
    to make me aware
That scattered profusely
    on life's thoroughfare
Are the best gifts of God
    that we daily pass by
As we look at the world
    with an unseeing eye.

Not to Seek, Lord, but to Share

Dear God, much too often
    we seek You in prayer
Because we are wallowing
    in our own self-despair . . .
We make every word
    we lamentingly speak
An imperative plea
    for whatever we seek . . .
We pray for ourselves
    and so seldom for others,
We're concerned with our problems
    and not with our brothers . . .
We seem to forget, Lord,
    that the "sweet hour of prayer"
Is not for self-seeking
    but to place in Your care
All the lost souls
    unloved and unknown
And to keep praying for them
    until they're Your own . . .
For it's never enough
    to seek God in prayer
With no thought of others
    who are lost in despair . . .
So teach us, dear God,
    that the power of prayer
Is made stronger by placing
    the world in Your care!

Prayers Can't Be Answered Unless They Are Prayed

Life without purpose
    is barren indeed—
There can't be a harvest
    unless you plant seed,
There can't be attainment
    unless there's a goal,
And man's but a robot
    unless there's a soul . . .
If we send no ships out,
    no ships will come in,
And unless there's a contest,
    nobody can win . . .
For games can't be won
    unless they are played,
And prayers can't be answered
    unless they are prayed . . .
So whatever is wrong
    with your life today,
You'll find a solution
    if you kneel down and pray
Not just for pleasure,
    enjoyment and health,
Not just for honours
    and prestige and wealth . . .
But pray for a purpose
    to make life worth living,

And pray for the joy
of unselfish giving
For great is your gladness
and rich your reward
When you make your life's purpose
the choice of the Lord.

God's Stairway

Step by step we climb day by day
Closer to God with each prayer we pray
For the cry of the heart offered in prayer
Becomes just another spiritual stair
In the heavenly staircase leading us to
A beautiful place where we live anew . . .
So never give up for it's worth the climb
To live forever in endless time
Where the soul of man is safe and free
To live in love through eternity.

You Helped Us Before,
God, Help Us Again

"O God, our help in ages past,
our hope in years to be"—
Look down upon this present
And see our need of Thee . . .
For in this age of unrest,
With danger all around,
We need Thy hand to lead us
To higher, safer ground . . .
We need Thy help and counsel
To make us more aware
That our safety and security
Lie solely in Thy care . . .
Give us strength and courage
To be honourable and true
Practising Your precepts
In everything we do,
And keep us gently humble
In the greatness of Thy love
So someday we are fit to dwell
With Thee in peace above.

God, Grant Us Hope and Faith and Love

HOPE for a world
    grown cynically cold,
Hungry for power
    and greedy for gold . . .

FAITH to believe
    when within and without
There's a nameless fear
    in a world of doubt . . .

LOVE that is bigger
    than race or creed,
To cover the world
    and fulfil each need . . .

    God, grant these gifts
    Of Faith, Hope and Love—
    Three things this world
    Has so little of . . .
    For only these gifts
    From Our Father above
    Can turn man's sins
    From hatred to love!

"On the Wings of Prayer"

Just close your eyes
      and open your heart
And feel your worries
      and cares depart,
Just yield yourself
      to the Father above
And let Him Hold you
      secure in His love—
For life on earth
      grows more involved
With endless problems
      that can't be solved—
But God only asks us
      to do our best,
Then He will "take over"
      and finish the rest—
So when you are tired,
      discouraged and blue,
There's always one door
      that is open to you—
And that is the door
      to "The House of Prayer"
And you'll find God waiting
      to meet you there,
And "The House of Prayer"
      is no farther away
Than the quiet spot
      where you kneel and pray—

For the heart is a temple
  when God is there
As we place ourselves
  in His loving care,
And He hears every prayer
  and answers each one
When we pray in His name
  "Thy will be done"—
And the burdens that seemed
  too heavy to bear
Are lifted away
  on the wings of prayer

Thank God for Little Things

Thank You, God for little things
  that often come our way—
The things we take for granted
  but don't mention when we pray—
The unexpected courtesy,
  the thoughtful, kindly deed—
A hand reached out to help us
  in the time of sudden need—
Oh make us more aware, dear God,
  of little daily graces
That come to us with sweet surprise
  from never-dreamed-of places.

A Prayer for Humility

Take me and break me and make me, dear God,
Just what you want me to be—
Give me the strength to accept what You send
And eyes with the vision to see
All the small arrogant ways that I have
And the vain little things that I do.
Make me aware that I'm often concerned
More with myself than with You,
Uncover before me my weakness and greed
And help me to search deep inside
So I may discover how easy it is
To be selfishly lost in my pride—
And then in Thy goodness and mercy
Look down on this weak, erring one
And tell me that I am forgiven
For all I've so wilfully done,
And teach me to humbly start following
The path that the dear Saviour trod
So I'll find at the end of life's journey
A home in the city of God.

Teach Us to Live

God of love—Forgive! Forgive!
Teach us how to truly live,
Ask us not our race or creed,
Just take us in our hour of need,
And let us know You love us, too,
And that we are a part of You . . .
And someday may man realize
That all the earth, the seas and skies
Belong to God who made us all,
The rich, the poor, the great, the small,
And in the Father's Holy Sight
No man is yellow, black or white,
And peace on earth cannot be found
Until we meet on common ground
And every man becomes a brother
Who worships God and loves each other.

Give Us Daily Awareness

On life's busy thoroughfares
We meet with angels unawares—
So, Father, make us kind and wise
So we may always recognize
The blessings that are ours to take,
The friendships that are ours to make
If we but open our heart's door wide
To let the sunshine of love inside

When Troubles Assail You
God Will Not Fail You

When life seems empty
And there's no place to go,
When your heart is troubled
And your spirits are low,
When friends seem few
And nobody cares
There is always God
To hear your prayers—
And whatever you're facing
Will seem much less
When you go to God
And confide and confess,
For the burden that seems
Too heavy to bear
God lifts away
On the wings of prayer—
And seen through God's eyes
Earthly troubles diminish
And we're given new strength
To face and to finish
Life's daily tasks
As they come along
If we pray for strength
To keep us strong—
So go to Our Father
When troubles assail you
For His grace is sufficient
And He'll never fail you.

"Now I Lay Me Down to Sleep"

I remember so well this prayer I said
Each night as my Mother tucked me in bed,
And today this same prayer is still the best way
To "sign off with God" at the end of the day
And to ask Him your soul to safely keep
As you wearily close tired eyes in sleep
Feeling content that the Father above
Will hold you secure in His great arms of love . . .
And having His promise that if ere you wake
His angels will reach down your sweet soul to take
Is perfect assurance that awake or asleep
God is always right there to tenderly keep
All of His children ever safe in His care
For God's here and He's there and He's everywhere . . .
So into His hands each night as I sleep
I commit my soul for the dear Lord to keep
Knowing that if my soul should take flight
It will soar to "The land where there is no night."